Math = Fun!™

Pizza Fractions

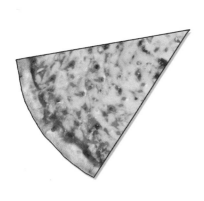

by Jerry Pallotta
Illustrated by Rob Bolster

SCHOLASTIC INC.

New York   Toronto   London   Auckland   Sydney
Mexico City   New Delhi   Hong Kong   Buenos Aires

Thank you to Dawn Colon of Hershey, Pennsylvania.
—Jerry Pallotta

This book is dedicated to Italian cooks.
—Rob Bolster

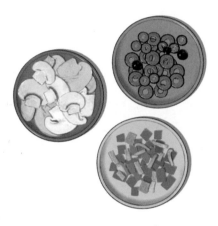

Text copyright © 2007 by Jerry Pallotta.
Illustrations copyright © 2007 by Rob Bolster.
All rights reserved. Published by Scholastic Inc.
SCHOLASTIC, Math = Fun!, and associated logos
are trademarks of Scholastic Inc.

ISBN-13: 978-0-545-00687-3
ISBN-10: 0-545-00687-2

12 11 10 9 8 7 6 5 4   10 11 12/0

Printed in the U.S.A.
This edition first printing, September 2007

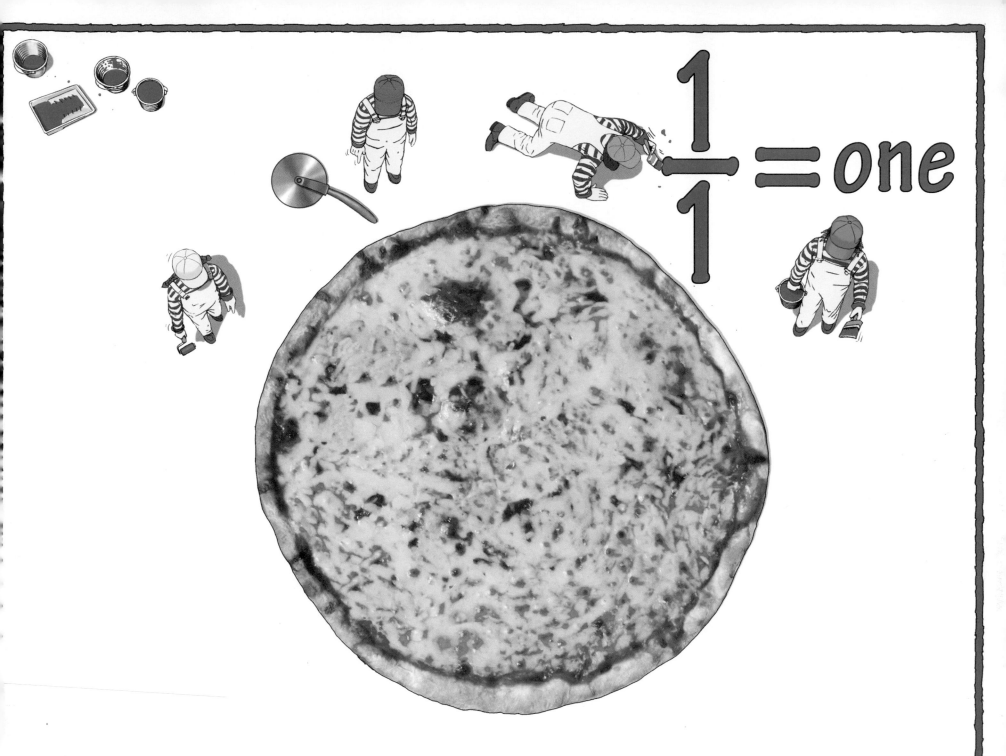

$$\frac{1}{1} = \text{one}$$

Here is a round cheese pizza. Pizza is one of the most popular foods in the world. Before we cut it into slices, we are going to learn about fractions.

The lunch ladies at school don't make round pizza.
They cook rectangular-shaped pizza.
Usually our pizza is topped with tomato sauce and cheese.

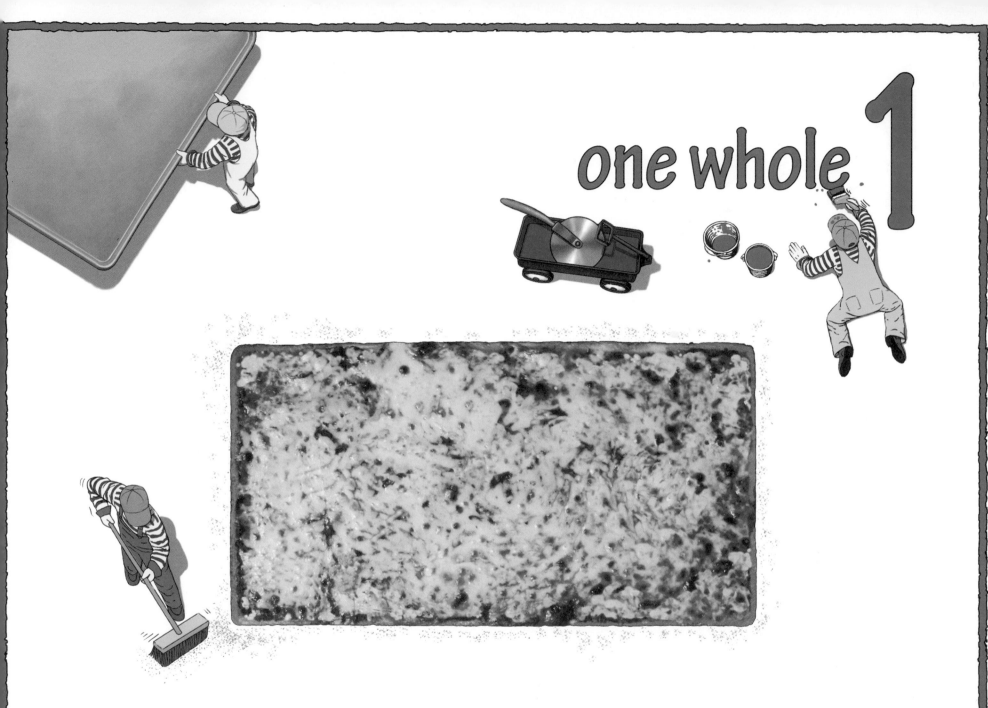

one whole 1

Here we have one whole cheese pizza.
And what is a fraction? A fraction is a part or portion of a whole thing.
We are using a rectangular-shaped pizza as our one whole thing.

$$\frac{12}{12}$$ twelve-twelfths

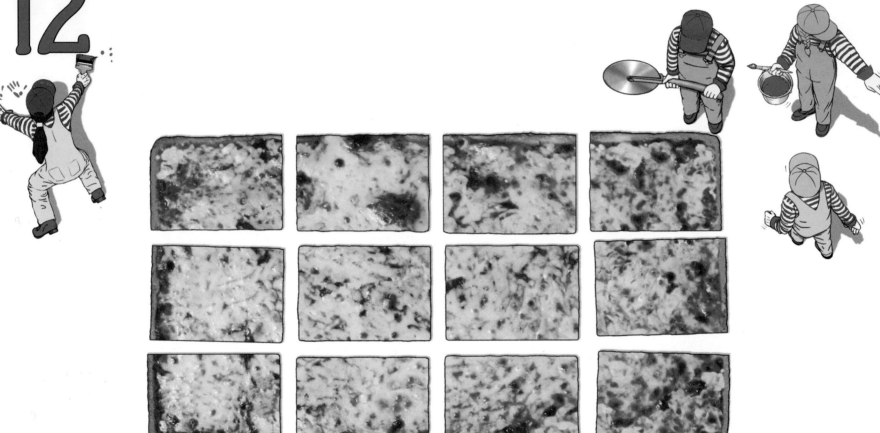

The lunch ladies slice this pizza into twelve equal sections.
One, two, three, four, five, six, seven, eight, nine, ten, eleven, twelve.

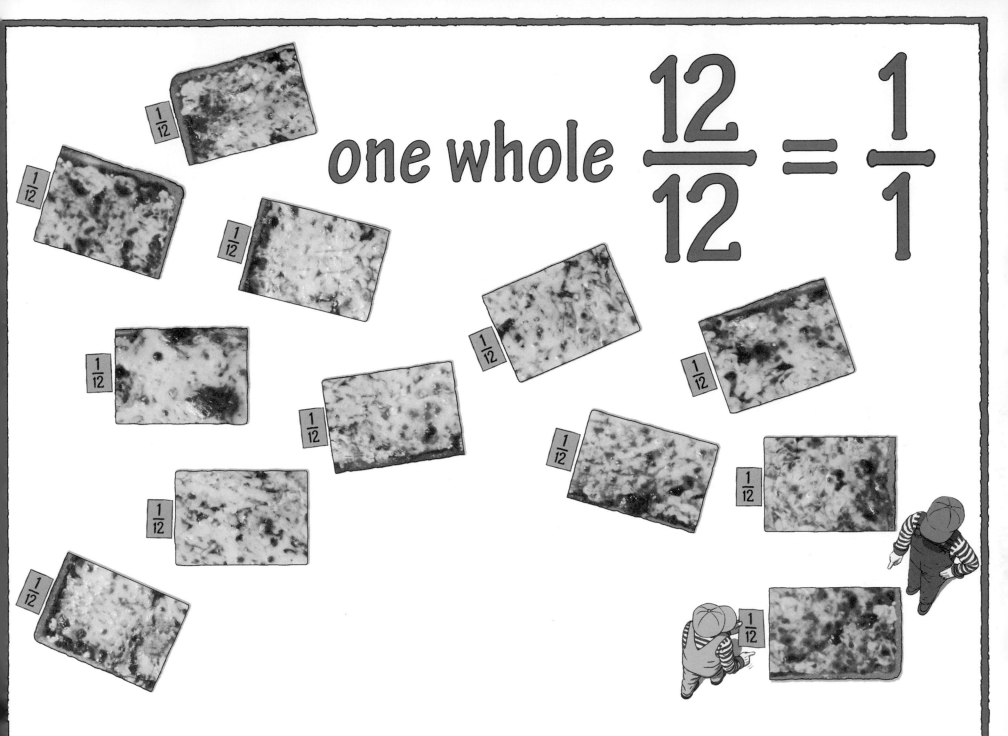

one whole $\dfrac{12}{12} = \dfrac{1}{1}$

You can rearrange the twelve equal slices any way you want.
Hey! It looks different, but they still equal one whole cheese pizza.

$$\frac{1}{12}$$ one-twelfth

Maybe this is the easiest way to understand fractions.
If your family was hungry, which would they rather eat?
One-twelfth of a cheese pizza?

eleven-twelfths $\frac{11}{12}$

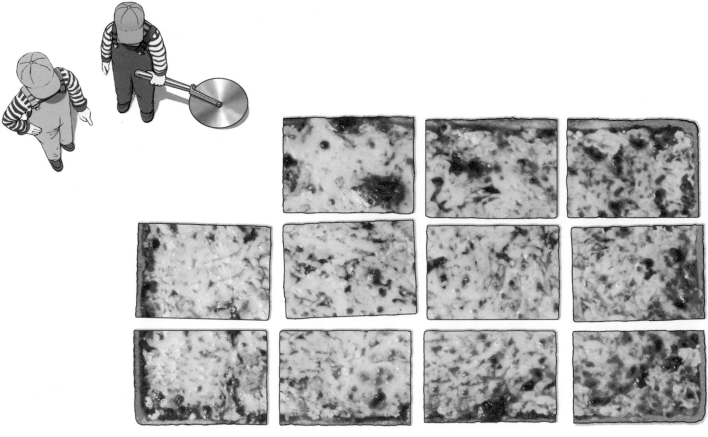

Or would they rather eat eleven-twelfths of a cheese pizza?
If you love pizza, the answer is simple.
As you can see, doing fractions can be fun.

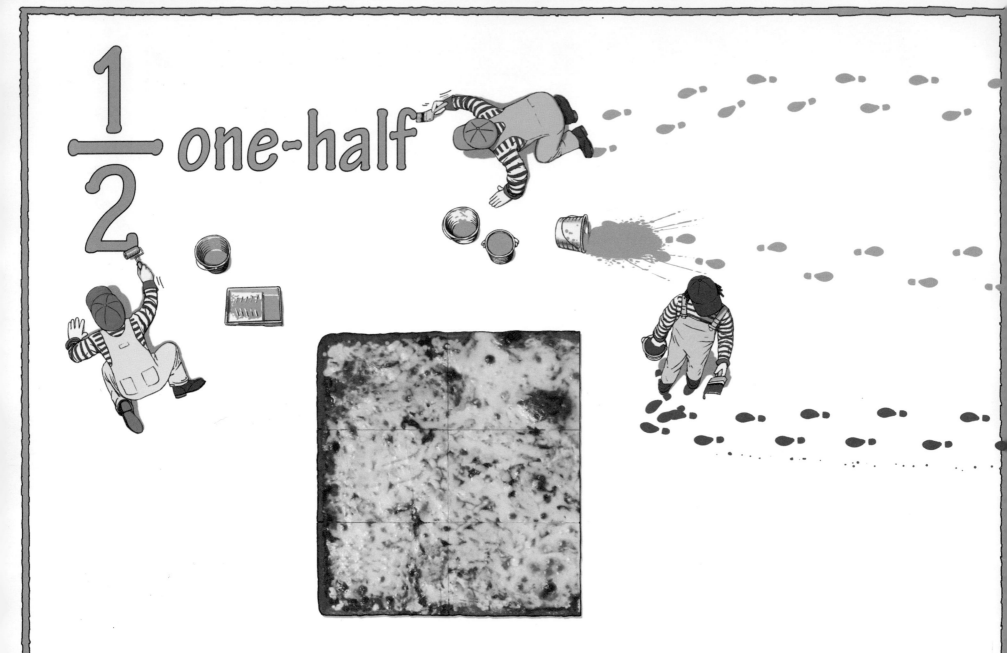

Here is one-half of the pizza.

six-twelfths $\frac{6}{12}$

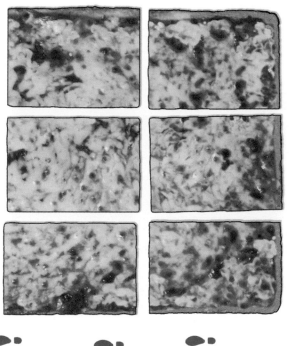

$$\frac{6}{12} = \frac{1}{2}$$

And here is the other half. Six-twelfths is equal to one-half.
When two fractions equal each other, they are called equivalent fractions.

$\dfrac{1}{3}$ one-third

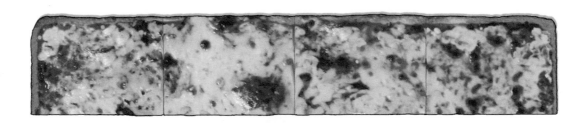

Here is one-third of a whole pizza. How did we get to the fraction of one-third?
Think of it like this: Our pizza can be divided into three equal groups.
Every one of the three groups has four equal slices.

two-thirds $\frac{2}{3}$

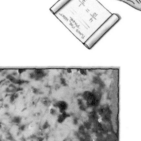

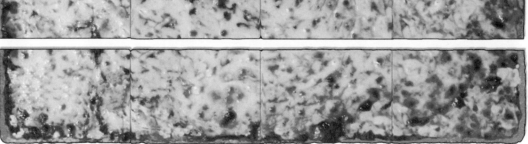

$$\frac{1}{3} + \frac{2}{3} = \frac{3}{3} = 1$$

What is left over is two-thirds. One-third plus two-thirds equals three-thirds.
When the top number and the bottom number are the same,
the fraction is equal to one.

$$\frac{4}{12}$$ four-twelfths

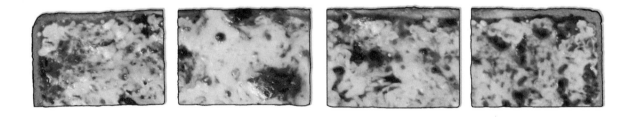

$$\frac{4}{12} = \frac{1}{3}$$

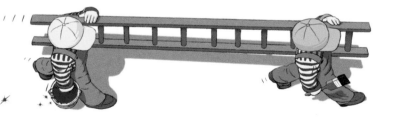

Here is another way of saying one-third. Four-twelfths is equal to one-third.

eight-twelfths $\dfrac{8}{12}$

$$\dfrac{8}{12} = \dfrac{2}{3}$$

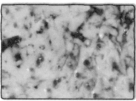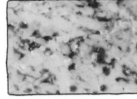

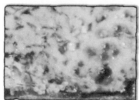

$$\dfrac{4}{12} + \dfrac{8}{12} = \dfrac{12}{12} = 1$$

And what is left over? Eight-twelfths.
Eight-twelfths is equal to two-thirds.
Four-twelfths plus eight-twelfths equals twelve-twelfths
which equals one whole pizza.

$\frac{1}{4}$ *one-fourth*

Here is one-fourth of a pepperoni pizza. We added another topping. If you want to call this fraction one-quarter, that is okay, too!

three-fourths $\frac{3}{4}$

$$\frac{1}{4} + \frac{3}{4} = \frac{4}{4} = 1$$

Here is what is left over: three-fourths.
You could call it three-quarters of a pepperoni pizza.

$\dfrac{3}{12}$ three-twelfths

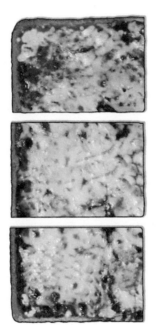

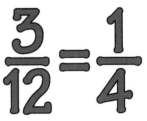

$$\dfrac{3}{12} = \dfrac{1}{4}$$

Three-twelfths is another way of saying one-fourth.
Did you know that the top number of a fraction is called the numerator and the bottom number is called the denominator? Now you know!

nine-twelfths $\dfrac{9}{12}$

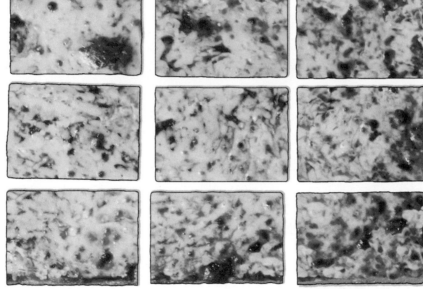

$$\dfrac{9}{12} = \dfrac{3}{4}$$

$$\dfrac{3}{12} + \dfrac{9}{12} = \dfrac{12}{12} = 1$$

Let's explain it another way.
Three-fourths is equal to nine-twelfths.

$\frac{1}{5}$ one-fifth

It's time for something different. We can still do fractions without the pizza. There are five cows on this page. Four cows have black spots and one cow has red spots. One-fifth of the cows on this page has red spots.

Did you ever wonder where cheese comes from? There is an easy answer. MILK! Cows give milk. Some of the milk is churned into cheese. Cheese is the most popular topping on pizza!

one-seventh $\frac{1}{7}$

If six cows *moo*ed, and you *moo*ed also, your *moo* would be one-seventh of all the *moo*s on this page. *Quack*! Don't forget to ignore the duck!

$$\frac{1}{6}$$ one-sixth

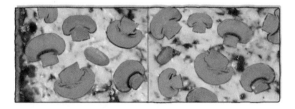

$$\frac{2}{12} \div \frac{2}{2} = \frac{1}{6}$$

Back to the pizza! This time we have a mushroom pizza.
We need to learn how to put a fraction into its lowest terms.
If you divide the numerator and the denominator by the same factor,
you can simplify this fraction to its lowest terms.
One-sixth is the lowest term of two-twelfths.

five-sixths $\dfrac{5}{6}$

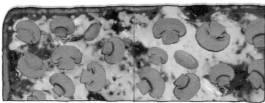 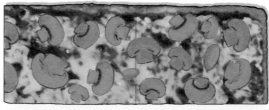

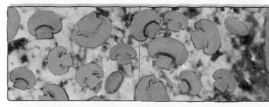

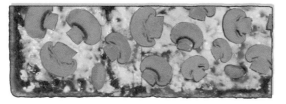 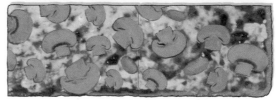

Five-sixths is what is left over from a whole mushroom pizza after removing one-sixth.

 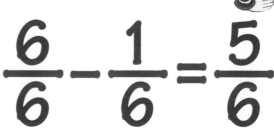

$$\frac{6}{6} - \frac{1}{6} = \frac{5}{6}$$

$$\frac{2}{12}$$ **two-twelfths**

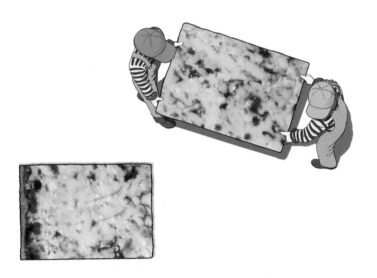

Here is an equation that is easy to understand.
One-sixth is equal to two-twelfths.

$$\frac{1}{6} = \frac{2}{12}$$

ten-twelfths $\dfrac{10}{12}$

Here's another way to say five-sixths: ten-twelfths.
Our school's pizza is starting to look more delicious after every fraction we show.

$\dfrac{1}{8}$ one-eighth

It's time for another break.
Tomato sauce is made by mashing tomatoes, adding spices, and cooking it.
Who makes the best sauce? The lunch ladies? Your nana? Or your mother?
Maybe your dad loves to cook.

one-ninth $\dfrac{1}{9}$

The sauce, cheese, and pizza dough are the three main ingredients used in making cheese pizza. The dough is made from flour. Flour comes from wheat. Here are nine stalks of wheat. If you cut down one stalk, you will have cut down one-ninth of the stalks of wheat on this page.

$\frac{5}{12}$ five-twelfths

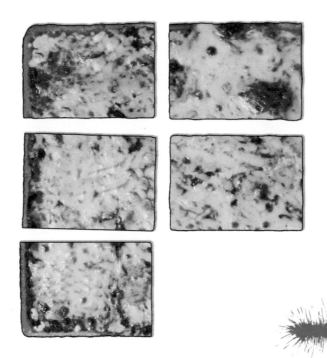

Here is an interesting fraction. It is already in its lowest terms.
The fraction five-twelfths cannot be broken down or reduced any further.

seven-twelfths $\dfrac{7}{12}$

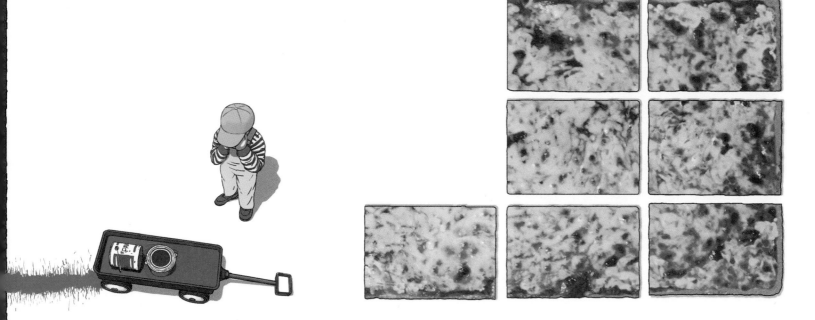

The amount left over from five-twelfths is seven-twelfths.
Seven-twelfths is another fraction that is in its lowest terms.

$\frac{1}{10}$ one-tenth

Here is a way to get a fraction of one-tenth.
One-tenth of the pizza boxes are open.

thirteen-twelfths $\frac{13}{12}$

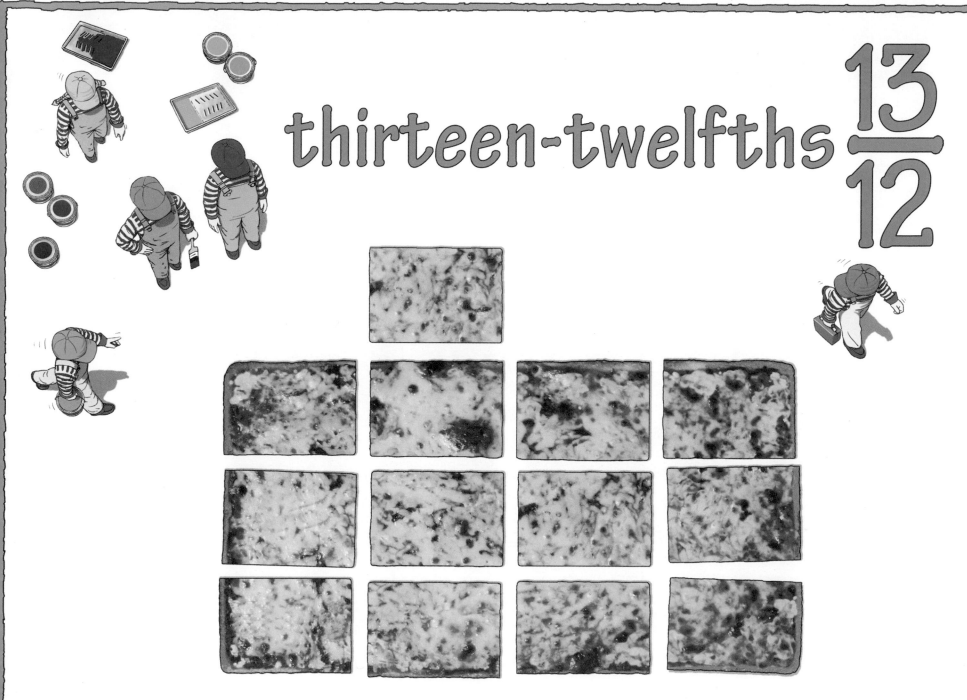

Here is a fraction where the top number is larger than the bottom number.
This is called an improper fraction. Thirteen-twelfths is really one and one-twelfth.
Whoever made this fraction used more than one pizza.

Now let's have some fun. Do some more fractions on your own.
Top your pizza with any of the following ingredients: olives, pepperoni,
onions, peppers, broccoli, mushrooms.
What fraction of every one did you use?